NATAL COMMAND

PHOENIX **POETS**

A SERIES EDITED BY ALAN SHAPIRO

PETER SACKS

Natal Command

THE UNIVERSITY OF CHICAGO PRESS

Chicago and London

Peter Sacks, a professor of English and American literature at Harvard University, was born in South Africa. He is the author of *The English Elegy: Studies in the Genre from Spenser to Yeats; Woody Gwynn: An Approach to the Landscape;* and two previous collections of poems, *In These Mountains* and *Promised Lands.*

The University of Chicago Press, Chicago 60637
The University of Chicago Press, Ltd., London
© 1997 by The University of Chicago
All rights reserved. Published 1997
Printed in the United States of America
06 05 04 03 02 01 00 99 98 97   1 2 3 4 5

ISBN: 0-226-73342-4 (cloth)
ISBN: 0-226-73343-2 (paper)

Library of Congress Cataloging-in-Publication Data

Sacks, Peter M.
    Natal command / Peter Sacks.
      p.   cm. — (Phoenix poets)
    ISBN 0-226-73342-4 (cloth : acid free paper)
    ISBN 0-226-73343-2 (pbk. : acid free paper)
    1. South Africa—Poetry.   I. Title.   II. Series.
PS3569.A235S9   1997
811'.54—DC21

97-5870
CIP

In Memory of My Father

Contents

Acknowledgments · ix

I The Gate · 3
   Natal Command · 4

II The Ridge · 31
    Night Ferry · 32
    May Eve · 33
    The Thorn · 35
    For Iris Hayter · 36
    Nuttall Gardens · 38

III Century · 41
     Kronos · 42
     Night Duty · 43
     Words · 44
     Judas Peak · 46
     Truce · 47
     Across the Field · 48
     Larkin · 50
     Drakensberg · 51

IV Kein Ander · 55

V Only the Swimmer · 67
   The Reins · 68

The Course · 69
Eclipse · 70
On the Path · 71
The Rock · 72
The Trench · 73
The Swimmer · 75
Blue Star · 77

Notes · 79

Acknowledgments

Versions of the following poems first appeared in these publications.

Boulevard: "Larkin," vol. 12, no. 3

Grand Street: "Kein Ander," *61: Identity,* vol. 16, no. 2; © Grand Street Press, 1997.

Harvard Review: "The Reins," "Eclipse," "The Swimmer," and prefatory poem as "Peter Sacks . . . so that in a new place," no. 12, Spring 1997

The New Republic: "Words" as "The Words"

Partisan Review: "Century" as "Hymn for the New Year," vol. LVI, no. 3, 1989; "Night Ferry," vol. LXIV, no. 3, 1997

Pequod: "Blue Star" as part of "Three Mourning Songs"

Seneca Review: "The Gate" as "Grieving" from *The Poet's Notebook: Excerpts from the Notebooks of 26 American Poets* (Norton, 1995)

Yale Review: "The Ridge" as "Aubade"

A black ship sails towards Pylos. The dolphin is huge, it comes at a rush and leaps from the dark water to the deck.

Immovable, heavier than bronze. Dazzling muscle of the sea. The sailors crouch back "silent and fearful." They shield their eyes.

The rocky coast of Pytho where the creature dives into the water, disappears, and comes back changed. "His long hair lay across his shoulders."

Shoreline, thin leaves turning to words: "And the altar itself shall be called Delphinian, Of-the-dolphin, overlooking everything."

Offshore, the sweet smell from the Bakers Biscuit factory. When the wind shifts south, a heavy stench of blubber from the whaling station at the far end of the bay.

I run for miles along draining glaze. Over tidelines. Hard sand runs beneath and through the body. Surf moves through (where now?) and breaks. The horse, the lion, the spray torn backward from waves.

Car lights coming on along the esplanade. The army camp. Hotels. The city sloping up to the Berea. Smoke from the "locations," Cato Manor, Kwa Mashu. The laws.

If they capture me I have not learned to speak.

I

The Gate

Silent I went out before dawn.
My life surged back until the field
lay buried in immeasurable light.

No world more real, for I was everywhere.

I too am dying. Where else can I be?

Natal Command

I.

Cross-hatchings, palm and rain,
   clapboard faded
to the grain, half-shutters
   open to old vines and mangroves

draining their own shadows;
    recollecting what the body knows
suspended between coral
    and shifting images of cloud . . .

     After death,
     after the knowledge
     of death,
     his death,

     his face, unwrapped,
     already yellowed,
     papery, recovered
     with a small white cloth

     then lowered away
     and shut to the earth;

So pierced,
so mute,
these words
re-opening:

Before. Not yet.
Not this.

*

2.

The rain had gone. I swam against the current,
harnessed by water till I turned and swung
out with the tide, shouldering deep

into a rhythm of my own, long strokes
pulled under the body and returning
past the glinting crease in which I breathed,

the sea half-woken like another body
bedded into sheer transparency,
the outer reaches granular with light.

Comebacks. Chains of radiance.
Far more than meet the eye.

What do they meet then, teasing, intimate
but otherworldly, mimicking the world?

        I looked back at the land's thin edge,
pines along the shoreline near a fort

where cannons rust, mouths left open among
thistleweed around the dozing moat.

Far back among fallen needles, pigeons shuffle
through shade, their feathers iris underlight,
soft flares bob the dark.

The land had disappeared.
The sun had followed it. From either wrist,
half-mingled with my breath into the night,

a trail of ungloved phosphor travelled back.

*

3.
Sounds too have their surfaces:

within
the mortal frame, particles of blood
revolve as in a sort of heaven where

breath moves through us as an unseen light;
but when the marrow bonds are parted they in turn
set loose what has been called the soul . . .

the spill and friction
glancing like a coin within a sea of coins;

my left hand pulls through as I breathe,
the right recovers, elbow in the air,

until the will behind the will strikes—
pike-flash in a swerving current,
predatory bird.

After death—his voice,
that constellation
shining out—

his face, his eyes—

as each had been, now

gone. Or going on,
a ghost—*another way*

*

4.

A slanting chop.

                       Erratic gasps
between thick chunks of water

crowded through the night.

The unclogged screw
    of a propellor

ringing into fossil-drillings,

detonations, manacles —

       (the jangled
       monkey-chain above his bed;

   he clung with both hands
     to the small trapeze,
   his lower body paralyzed
     for months . . .

           not this)—

     far larger than myself,
      a shambling hulk,

        tentacular, a pulpy
   helmet, lantern eyes,
     the huge mouth gorging,

undigested corpses
bulging in the belly wall.
I thrashed to break free

but the ocean held me,
and a slap of water broke
across my mouth.

*

5. Natal Command

Troughs of recollection; hands now two numb sponges,
and a cold ache pressed into the spine.

A conscript leaning on my rifle, I stood guard for hours
staring through wire toward the Blue Waters Hotel:

an all-night crew, unreal, fluorescent
polished the lobby floors; high in a yellow cell

black shadows rippled on drapes until the lights went out.
The sentry's solitude. The muffled crump of surf

beyond the esplanade; the ocean shifting
to an onshore drowse of salt over the palm trees and camp.

A palm rat slithers through rotten fronds.
The mind floats imageless.

Then back to footage of commandos stalking a sentry
from behind—the pounce, a hand clamped hard

over the mouth, the blade thrust in, the sagging weight set down,
a clutch to save the helmet as it drops to gravel, quick

hand signals to shadows hunched behind. One night while
still on guard I crept into an empty tent and fell asleep.

The duty sergeant found me—legs stuck out beneath the flap.
He held my rifle. Prodded the bayonet at my spine,

"Keep sleeping and they'll kill us all," he whispered
as the bayonet found the nerve, pain jolting

to my hands and feet. His boot beside the blade
he pumped me hard against the ground then let me up,

my limbs still trembling, the uniform stuck bloody to my back.

*

6.

        When does it begin,
submission sliding into savagery—
the reptile mind among its enemies

revenged and striking—bayonet
driven deep into the bag,

the rifle stock slammed home,
the scream in my own mouth?

        A guard dog chained
against the fence.
The collar chokes it back.

*

7.

When I was eight our Latin master had us stand beside him
while he marked our work. The desk concealed us below

the waist and he'd reach up our shorts to run his hand
along the inside of our thighs. Shift or step away

he'd growl "Stand still!" or "Pay attention, boy!"
as if his fondling were the lesson.

Sacks-and-bags he called me; and one afternoon, my eyes
fixed on an ink stain at my feet, the wood floor rocking

like a ship—*navis, navem*—willing myself out of it,
out of the room, out of the body, swaying in the heat

but also silken, wondering, astray, near fainting
as the nausea heaved—I threw up on his head.

A half-digested avocado in a mess of milk. Fumbling
for his handkerchief he wiped his face, his scalp,

his glasses, "Alright Sacko never mind; can you get down
to sick bay on your own or should I send the Bishop with you?"

Walking home I stopped to watch a line of men work on the road.
They swung their pickaxes in unison, the sun caught flashing

as they poised axe heads for a moment overhead, then with
a slow arc slammed them down into the asphalt crust:

overalls stripped to the waist, cloth arms dangling
near their legs, they chanted out what may have been a long

insult against the foreman, the *umlungu,* lounging, shirt
unbuttoned, pale belly gleaming in the shade. The work song

hoisted, held mid-phrase, the weight of it, then driven
with a hard expulsion of breath into the ground.

*

8.

The will is broken,
realigned, then broken further,

burning like another
spine within the spine.

A sentry-spy,
it stalks us from behind.

The sunken path emerges
not as feeling nor as thought

but as the mind itself,
historical, embodied, and alive.

*

9.
                    Forgotten nights,

the shuck and wash of tides,
entangled shadows of the burglar guards

sent wriggling on the blanket as I stirred there
sleepless, sickened by the swirling

mind lured outward into unknown pleasures
swarming back against the fear

of punishment, of being maimed,
of others' injuries . . .

        Bright red, page after page,
my father's medical thesis,
                            my fingers
pressing small black corners
into which he slid the photographs,

the gloss unbuckling,
                    Now look away

(I was no more than five), but what I saw
each time if only for a second, stares at me:

More than naked—
cut apart or sewn;
encrusted. Swollen,
unknown organs

sectioned off
but spilling into
sight—
unframed.

Enormous.
More than any body
could be made to bear.

It was a drowning agony,
compassion sinking
into anger, shame, disgust,
resurging with each later shock

      —the dead flesh
grafted on a classmate's arm
held close against my face
until I hunched down pleading
for release;

        the veteran on the bus,
half-seen, then fully seen,
a boiled mask stretched tight
and welded to the head;

  the sugar-worker's hand
crushed by the mill—a red
stump held up to the car,

blood on the lowering glass.

No other way.

As through a single
wound ripped past
all dressing—

reaching further in

*

10.

We tried to bathe him, dabbing,
sponging as he crouched above
the bathroom floor;

then carried him,
                but weakly,
terrified to grip too hard,
new fractures in the shoulders,
skin like tissue tearing

in my hands—

                a slow nightmarish
stumble to the bed,
he almost slipping free.

Never so powerless,
exchanging that one glance.

The stuff between us acrid,
clogging, unexpungeable

as he lay back, *Thanks boy,*
against the bloodied sheet.

No other words beside the pulsing,
mortal, mortal, mortal, mortal.

                *

II.

Above a splotch of green far down against the wrinkled
blue—but nothing under me no wing no craft no seat

only flapping pages of *The Mercury* on which I squatted
knowing if I clutched I'd fall but grabbing as the papers

tore and lofted and I fell back to the water rushing
at me—following the dream through schools of eels

lampreys hagfish one-eyed flounders polyps nameless
weeds descending fathom after fathom to a buried apex

body taken up into the mind impacted grinding
through the ocean bed into the core—a drill bit

whirling every splinter bone chip ion of the self
disintegrating through a blowhole into nothingness

the water sucked away the air evacuated and the thought
of any form—face shoulders torso pelvis legs—

*

12.

How long could it have been before the thickening
of spine and brain, the limbs' recovered
grappling through old fears, old anger

buried in the reef, whole chunks ripped upward
clinging to the arms, the rusted throat worked loose,
a still unbroken grief approaching as for air?

As ripples move across a pool before there is a pool,
so after nothing that I could perceive, an origin
of light moved out into another version of itself

and I was driven with it to a vertical horizon—
wall or contour of a high inhuman skull, opaquely veined,
through which I saw a river branching into cataracts.

Light beaten into sound, sound blown and beaten into light,
a river-tree held up between its planetary leaves
huge cysts and spores of darkness casting out

bright shocks that spiralled to the widest
limits of the wall. The force reverberated through
all sheathing, drawing elemental shapes out of the field

where they stirred, magnetic, crystalline,
the salt and grains of dust converging into gravity
around me, rotated and gathered toward the shore.

*

13.

Continuance,
the measure of
continuance;

gray shell,
blood-red anemone,
my hands,

my shoulders,
found, resumed,
permissible.

Re-oriented
oarings; sifted
semi-tropic

scatterings,
unsearched
till now

contending,
charged with
gravity

(*once more*),
remorseless
from the broken

cell—no
reason in but
of the law,

too many
particles
(*it was no*

offering)
to pronounce
. in time.

*

14.
(From the Train, near Anzio, Veterans Day 1994)

Out of the body comes intelligible speech,
but from such wordlessness as if the body
were the world. Leaning out, my hand

against the sill, I watched wild poppies flare
along the track, the cinders whispering *here they are,*
they are . . . too many to be held in sight,

red poppies blurring out of recollection,
seeping back, reopened, flattened to crepe
petals pinned against our uniforms in school.

The shallow pride of decorations worn
against my terror even at photographs
of war; seen once, a *Life* or *Look* left open

to a soldier blasted to a ragged mess.
For years when I went up alone to bed
he ambushed me: across the darkened landing,

left arm flailing, right crammed down
against the entrails, head torn open,
mouth near-gone and one eye left to stare

fast glazing out the last thing it would see,
my own hand scrabbling up the wall toward
the light switch that would blank him out.

What did I fear beyond the quick blood-soaked
immersion through the living and the dead—
as if by diving through a single swell

I could resurface out behind the lines,
a momentary calm in which another
wave returns still higher, thicker, lunging

overhead from the horizon—crying out—
so that I press my hand over the shattered
mouth, our bodies wrestle intertwined,

his writhing under mine, a swirl of weed,
red fish, red blossoms gathered, mounded,
breaking into flight then gathering again

until at last remaining what it was
—the human form, no more no less
however torn, opposing everything:

"Control yourself and listen. All you know
is words, *the other than*. Why do you think
your father never spoke of it? Can you imagine

what it's like to watch a thousand sheep
stampeded through a minefield into enemy fire;
then stumbling across that field yourself,

haystacks burning, blood and chaos everywhere,
you hear your friend yell, *Watch your hairnet
dearie*! then his head explodes beside you

in a splash of brains and hair the bloody
muck over your mouth your eyes your ears?"
—I answered nothing. Neither death

nor dying but my body's own first
certainty of butchery had ruptured
through me: my life against his own,

against his life *and* death to which
no word, no year of words could count
for more than an evasion pressing back

toward an image of the dead recovered,
grappled, conjured into life
—or banished wholly out of mind.

I knew there'd be no end to this betrayal.
The same aftershock by which he vanished
rippled now behind my eyes, and through the words

your mouth your eyes your ears the bloody muck
and through each breath itself until
these too rushed backward with the track,

the stones, the cinders, the innumerable poppies
bending back and shaken as we passed.

II

The Ridge

Slow dawn. The rain diffused to hang as steep
mist draped across the meadow and far trees.
The silence balanced, stirred yet still asleep
between birdcalls—their first unyielding clarities.

Night Ferry

Blood-drop, lung of fire setting past
the sea bell and wave; why am I separate
from that giant burrowing into further life?

The body breathes and rides
a heavy-netted ocean swollen
by the tide. Under the half-moon

it's the lighthouse light that turns
the rest of me to early nightfall,
headland, home. I send it back,

a mirrored flickering across cold waters.
We allow ourselves the crest that breaks
above the surface then re-forms.

We make it human and we call it love.
This wintering is my own and not the world's,
although the world is wintering.

May Eve

Squatting forward, balancing, you shift
the spade in your right hand, a plastic tray
beside your left, both heels lifted

from your sandals, black skirt drawn tight
across your knees. You're planting annuals:
pansies colored like lake shallows lightly

overlapping their own deeper blues,
poppies and dark violets with a smudge
of nightfall at the core. You press each cube

of root soil down into bone meal and dirt,
your body's weight pressed into the earth.
Whose breath is it, the drifting air still

riding out as twilight shines again
upon its fading? Under leaf and stalk
the garden stirs upon its bed of shade,

the buds unfold a scent released yet driven
back into each recess of the flower.
—And how else can I speak to you of love

so clenched my heart and yet so overridden
by this joy, forever lost then felt and lost
until the earth itself becomes the million-

petalled blossom opening its center
to the darkest reaches of night?
O love, your face turned listening for a sound

half-gone but rising still between the soil
and garden air—come closer: there's
no part of us that will survive this flowering.

The Thorn

Ah blackbird, giving thanks
from your nest in the thorn. . . . Hermit
that use no bell: soft, sweet,
from the otherworld, your whistle!

The words belong to every other life,

new branches glitter at the edge
of an impartiality that never once was ours.

Where do we store sensation,
and our early urgings where are they?

It's within reach, you think, that joy—
unhidden, on the inside, giving it away.

For Iris Hayter (on Her 80th Birthday)

Edges of the field hold the shadow
and the shadow holds the eye. Half-open
door, old heart and chimney place—
out of the empty stable of oaks
dark horses shift the early issuance
of evening to the unlit earth, whose horses
move across the field and are the field
itself, the full returning weight of it.

I've heard of horsemen in the Asian steppes
who carry drum charts of the spirit's
journey—pathways drawn into the hide
stretched tight over a cylinder of air;
tapping finger or heel of hand,
the body sounded against nothingness
like footfalls of another life, a beating
heart's own shadow passing through.

That summer we drove out at dusk and stopped
near Beckley where a sloping pasture gathered
afterlight but for a cleft of woods,
near-charcoal in the depths. The moon drew
from the hill behind us like another
hillside gradually set free, its smoky
copper burning clear, already bright
as we drove back Woodperry Drive.

It was there in the long avenue a single
black horse leaned toward us through the limes,
the moonlit neck leaf-shadowed and the head
almost entirely lost among leaves.
The stillness held toward a deepening
impression of itself until the night
was filled with it, a large horse
standing quietly among trees.

We carry our own spirit with us and at times
the given world becomes the spirit's world.
By winter you had written, "Autumn
hasn't blown away as much as usual—"
another season in which every loss
is more than what the spirit chooses to let go.
The nomad knows it, and the gardener.
Whoever passes and will not return.

Nuttall Gardens

Working hour after hour, the mind and senses
blurred, absorbed, almost asleep;

and then the trowel grates against
a stone, the clash sent shivering

back into the arm, neck, skull.
You set it by, you work now with your hands

until they are two flowers turning in the soil;
everywhere you bend you find sediments

of root and leaf, old marrow-fleck and mineral,
a blunted stem, a sinking glint of bone

—from years below, the unforgotten
surplus cast ahead of us into the dirt.

III

Century

Thrown back, the headless
rooster flails the ground,
the final spasm of its wing
beats through the compound

where we shelter—reaching
this time for the fat black hen,
its feathers fouled with panic
—saying *These too were given*

for our hunger: water; fire;
the tree of which we made
this level stump;
and iron for the blade.

Kronos

Strip back the metal psalms
to your charred battleground,
the single body welded shut,
disaster-crowned.

Spread-eagled trench by trench
the earth lies on its bed;
—whose aftercry will sow
your melancholy seed?

Unnatural father each new
love defies until it too
is swallowed in the forge,
ring out your pig-iron lullabies!

Night Duty

Red oasis,
reddened palms,

a row of stumps
still soak

through gauze.
We move in silence,

the undreaming white
ghosts, whispering.

If not for love, I hate.
I hate my kind.

Words

In Memory of T. Carmi

Jerusalem, *the stone of losses,*
near as my right hand.

The beauty of the earth
that was not also torn away.

The tree whose branches
run over the wall.

A choking laughter
between breaths,

the smoke of Europe rising
in an unfamiliar light.

The crease around the eyes
for obstinacy, courage,

and their opposites still faltering
between the mortar and flesh.

The blood like nightfall
that will not be lifted from dust;

and you now part of it forever,
word for word, repeatable—

there is no other city for the dead.

Judas Peak

The wars were in another country then.
My hair is whitening. Under the lamp

I clenched my fist until the veins made up
a false map legible across the wrist.

Call me what you want—stone fin, hatchet-heart;
each new face ripped to pieces at my base.

Truce

Tasting it.

Mute dunes, your skull,
another's hands.

Croak not black angel
I've no food for you.

Only this
mockery—

after the ghosts
go down—

of unspent
breath.

Across the Field

Do you write for catharsis?
Should we read that way?

*

A faith in works, A faith in works.
And further back: *Stripped to the bone!*

*

A shadow skims the grass,
sight tracks upward

skittering till it's caught
and carried by a hawk—already braking

hard to settle on the dead arm of an oak.

*

Wind roughs up the feathers but the branch
rocks with such regularity

the bird's sway balances the tree.

*

The long wide-angled gaze breaks off.

One apprehension
locks against another, stiffening.

*

Yesterday, a ring of yellow
feathers in the leaves; and nothing

but a shinbone of the finch,
the claw intact.

Larkin

Pull back the lining of the normal thought.
Black moss. Old brick. Lopsided moon.
O Truth; O Grief; O Clarity! O.K.
Again. This time let's get it right.
The only memory worth savoring—
Your sour breath against the pane,
Wiped clearer for it—bright, unwavering.

Drakensberg

The branch was jagged, charred by mountain fires,
twisted on itself by wind and river water,

but I reach for it again out of the rush and swirl,
my hand clenched fast, the wet bark giving its own

grip under the glistening. Shafts of new leaves,
long-tongued, leathery. A single protea hanging

low, the cup of pink and black fur
bracketed with interlocking petals to the rim.

Tight-packed, the seethe and drench of it.
And every other part of me still dragged away.

IV

Kein Ander

Paul Celan (1920–1970)

you island-meadow
you yourself
fogged in with
hope

Against
the
fence

of our
own
century

— too much
ash to
bless —

we follow
gray
thread

finger-
splitting

bits
of
bolt & barb

the furnace
stars downriver
to

another
song
the singer's

hand caught
brighter
than a red rag in

the wire

       *

loosestrife
forget-me-nots
cut

& bound to
wheat
shocks

your body
thrown
between

the blind
man at the mill
enslaved

& a thawing
gutterful
of vowels

half-ground
against
the end—

one black one
reddening
one red

        *

out of
the battering
wheel

each spoke
another
rivulet

sheared off
between
high stone

hedges
of the Seine

the knife
resharpened
bodies

stacked
the
threshing

stone
your chest
ripped

shivering
from
depths

*

the rose

of wire
knotted
sharp enough

to memorize
the hand for
once

as once
the bird
leaned all

night long
against
the thorn

*

behind
the hanging
veil

each last
child swept
downriver

looking back—

the mother
muttering
but listen

listen
too afraid
to hide is

taken out
& shot

a bullet
in the neck

*

& he
that singeth
hard against

the wire
sang
he sang

*

all-spending
river

we too
drag him
through folds

of feldspar
metagraywacke
gneiss

plutonic magma
buckled
to our own

horizon
riven past
invention

& remade

*

the bridge
falls upward
splinters

in the mind
—it is the
force

beneath
the words
that drives

through death
the stiffened
silence

travels
past the river
mouth

the white-
lipped
sea rebuffs

& crushes in
the old
salt quarry

where
the words
whirl out

     *

implacable

brought near
engraved
volcanic

schist
stripped
back to

stone bees
in the flint
the wings

unbroken
barely
tarnished

nibs
of pollen
glimmering

     *

one for
many

none

the early
vessel crazed
by images

of earthly
fire
the almond

blossom
strung
ignited by

our thirst
word after
pouring

word thrust
further
downward

—*you*
wedged
headlong

deep into
the crown
of roots

no other

seed no
scratch
of light

        *

your throat

torn through
the soiled
waters

        *

torn away

v

Only the Swimmer

He can't forget them:
night, the swimmer and the words
 Only the swimmer. . . .

Night swims, the swimmer
passes between stars that drop
  below the surface

of the words for nightfall,
and the words swim.
  Darkening they glide.

After long pauses
they begin again. *Only*
  the swimmer stays down.

The Reins

Many are the faces pressed against the wind,
strong is the wheel of heat, the ungloved hand.

Out of the cliff you made the fountain,
out of flint the dolphin in the wave;

why should you fear us—knowing how the cloth
slid from her body, her mouth opened to my own

—unless desire is infinite, each particle
from the beginning driven from you

forcing its intolerable weight into the world.

The Course

No one on the horizon until you.

You say you once came nearer. Where was I?
What was I listening for?

So headlong under cloud the driven rain.

The blunt stone of the world turns in your hand.

Eclipse

Our moonlit breath. At every moment
vanishing; but such a weight remains.

Now you are closer you say, do not
let me die though we move into death.

I answer following, keep as our own
the light cast out between our shadows,

and that further shining out
beneath the disappearing shadow of the earth.

On the Path

This morning on the path
the word *bereft* broke open:

Calm yet easily startled, cautious,
strenuous at work, yet laughing,

cresting, loving beauty,
beautiful yourself — elate.

I thought there would be greater
knowledge in the end.

The Rock

We hardly touched.

A parched kiss on the lips
too brief to drink.

Be absolute you said,
we are not free.

*

Pitch-dark, so pitched,
the lines flare out.

The night broke open
to excess, the rock

at high tide drenched
by each returning wave.

God, how it shines from you!

The Trench

Only disembodied senses serve us here.
Or are there other senses too insatiable for death?

*

You waited on the stairs but moved
to keep me still in sight.

Whoever I was then saw nothing
but your face, your hand, the storm door

closing till you sank within a mirrored sky
and I could barely lift my eyes to the glass.

What looked through us before you turned away
burns through the hard mask of the world.

*

I lost my glove, drawn off
to write of you.

Above the waves a voice
called out for words beyond my hearing

and it was your voice. The sun sank
like the red stone wheel of the season.

Though I cannot see it now it points to you.

The Swimmer

You said you never turned toward me
as I turned to you. That island

in the west is no new world.
But think of love:

even the surface unreceived,
the whole horizon lifted to a single

flame cast out against the water's weight,
your arms, your hands, your face

held close above the waves.
I knew I'd never see you in that way again

and that was death—the salt torn off,
the senses ripped back out of life.

*

Below the cliff's edge voices still pursue us.
When I broke the surface after *I would love to,*

you asked, *Which way are you swimming now?*—
the joke behind the high white laughter

off the rocks, the same explosion.
Spine-stack, skull,

the arm bones fallen forward
to the scattered hand.

Out of air, out of the offshore wind
the words reopen their own senses,

reaching for another breath, your breath.

Blue Star

That day the west
burned like a sheet of ice crazed
by the tree's black hammerblow.

Dark arteries,
there's nothing stronger
than my own surviving hunger.

But the sky said
Break now or be broken.

         *

Blue star. And the star
fell westward drawing
the last daylight from
the field's edge.

My own translation took me deeper,
star of both hemispheres.
Past the low stone wall of the horizon,
owl-dark and the bloodbeat of its wing,

I could hear everything,
For you must break a grief

to mend it. The body's
work song and the heavy spade

divided light and shade
from what is neither light nor shade;
and life flocked forward,
hungering and feeding at the verge.

Notes

"Natal Command"

    Natal Command is the name of a military camp in Durban, in the
    province of Natal (pronounced Natál), South Africa.

"The Thorn"

    Epigraph, Thomas Kinsella's translation of the anonymous Gaelic poem
    from the tenth century.

"Words"

    T. Carmi (1925–1994), Israeli poet, one of whose collections was trans-
    lated under the title *At the Stone of Losses*.

"Judas Peak"

    Judas Peak is an outcrop of the Cape Peninsula in South Africa.

"Drakensberg"

    The Drakensberg is a mountain range in South Africa.

"Kein Ander"

    "No Other." Epigraph from the poet Nelly Sachs (1891–1970) in a letter
    to Paul Celan. Celan, whose parents were killed by the Nazis, took his
    life by jumping from a bridge into the Seine.